Will you cross a BRIDGE?
Color Me BRIDGE

Katherine A. Simons

Parson's Porch Books

Will You Cross a BRIDGE? Color Me BRIDGE

ISBN 978-1-946478-51-1   Softcover

All rights reserved. No part of this book may be reproduced or transmitted in any form or by any means, electronic of mechanical, including photocopying, recording or by any information storage system without permission in writing from the publisher.

To order additional copies of this books, contact:

Parson's Porch Books 1-423-310-8815

www.parsonsporch.com

Parson's Porch Books is an imprint of Parson's Porch & Company (PP&C) in Cleveland, Tennessee an innovative company which raises money by publishing books of noted authors, representing all genres. All donations from contributors and profits from publishing are shared with the homeless.

For Mairn

Introduction

Will you cross a BRIDGE? Color me BRIDGE is a life question in response to a story in Genesis about Noah, and Paul's life question told in a letter to the Galatians. People can take action building a BRIDGE thru Presbyterian Disaster Assistance (pda.pcusa.org) by:

    Coloring Talking
    Reflecting
    Receiving
    Giving

Learning BRIDGES all

Peace,
Katherine A. Simons

Will You Cross a *BRIDGE?* Between

Will you Cross a BRIDGE? Color me BRIDGE

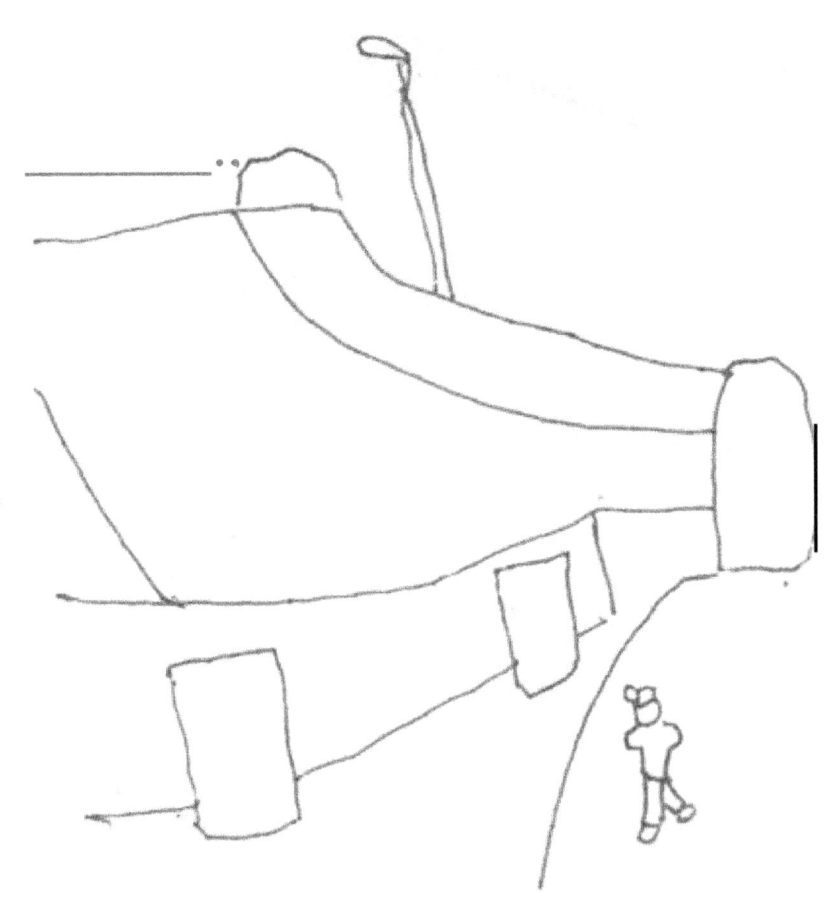

Will you Cross a **BRIDGE**?

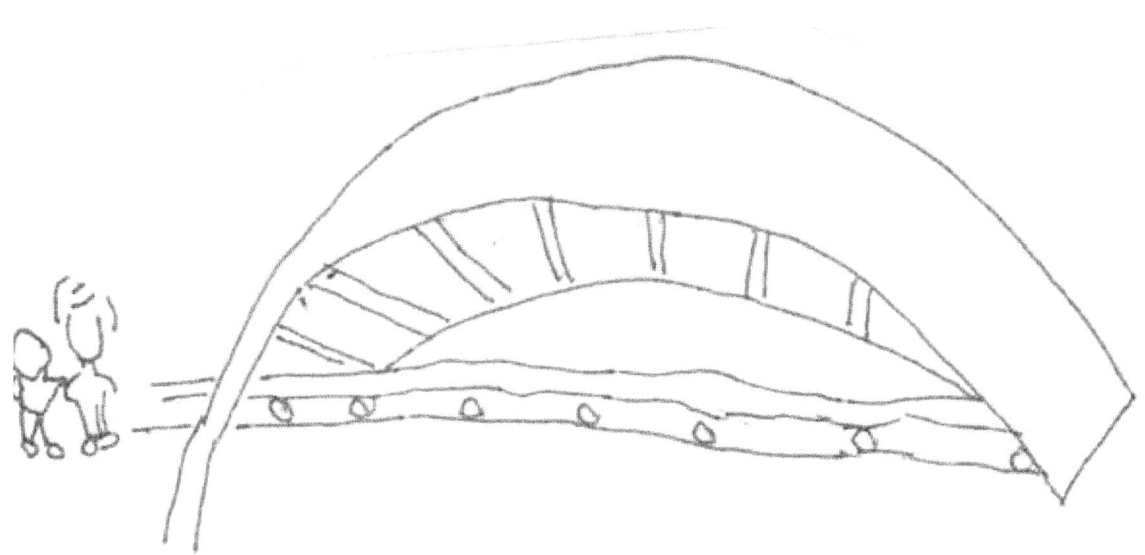

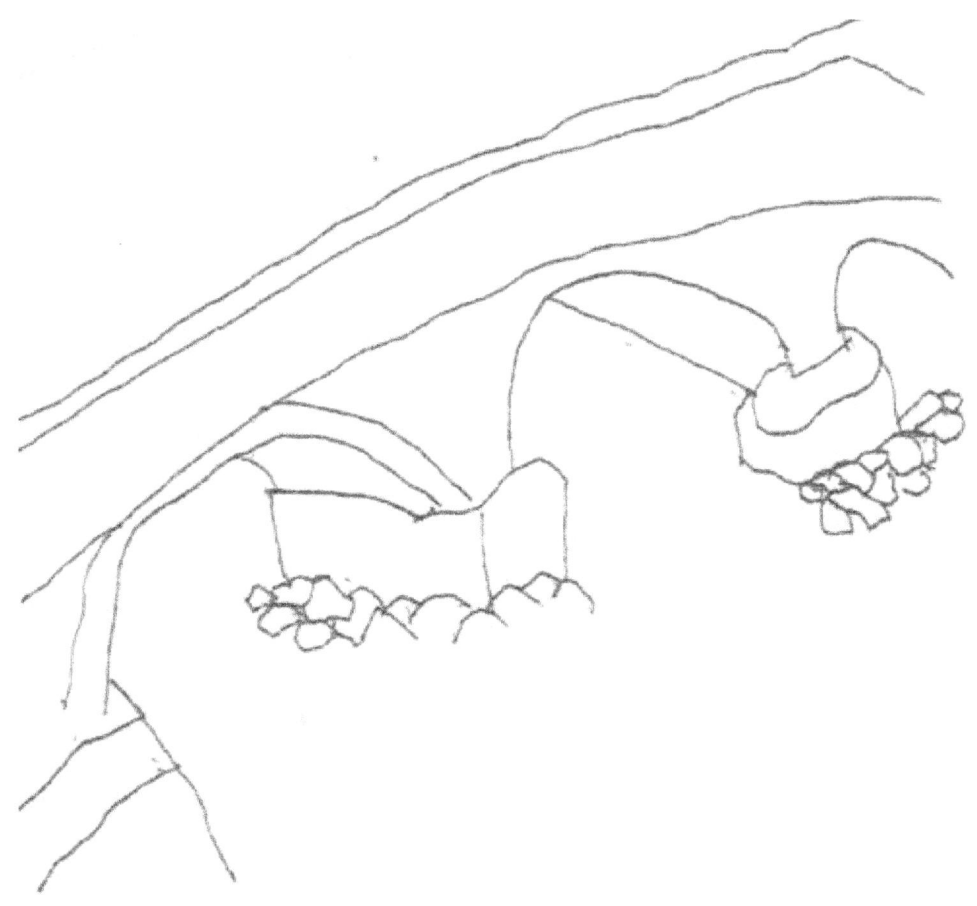

God said,

"I set my bow in the cloud, And it shall be a sign of the covenant Between me and the earth" Genesis 9.13

Will you cross a BRIDGE? Color me BRIDGE

Will you Cross a BRIDGE? Color me **BRIDGE**

Will you Cross a BRIDGE? Color me BRIDGE

Will you Cross a BRIDGE? Color me BRIDGE

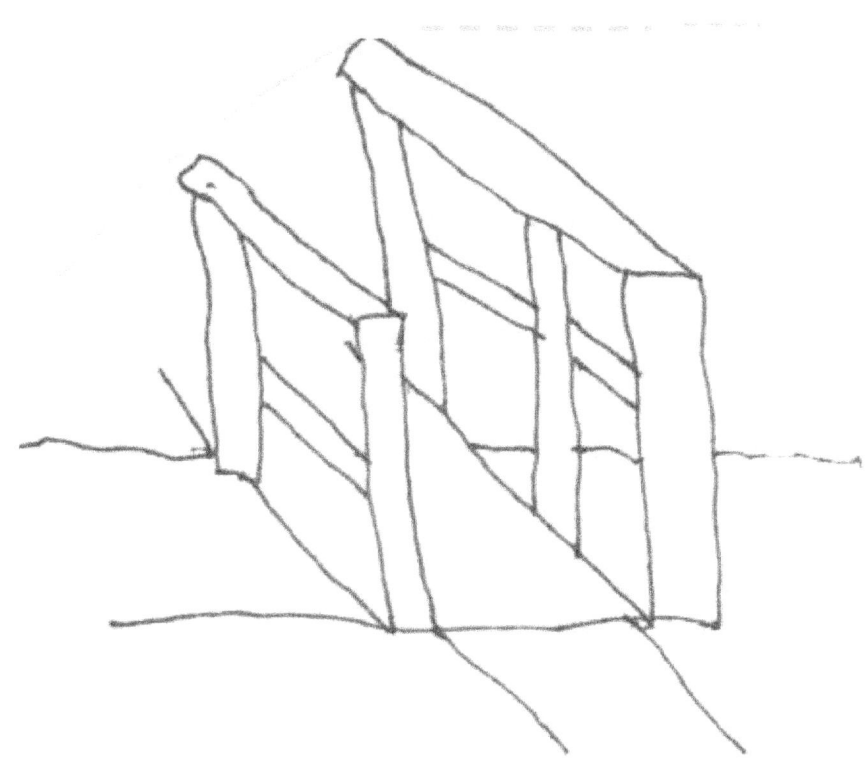

Will you cross a BRIDGE? Color me BRIDGE

Paul writes to the people in Galatia:

"There is neither Jew nor Greek,
There is neither slave nor free, There
is neither male nor female,
For you are all one in Christ Jesus" says God.

Galatians 3.28

Will you Cross a BRIDGE? Color me BRIDGE

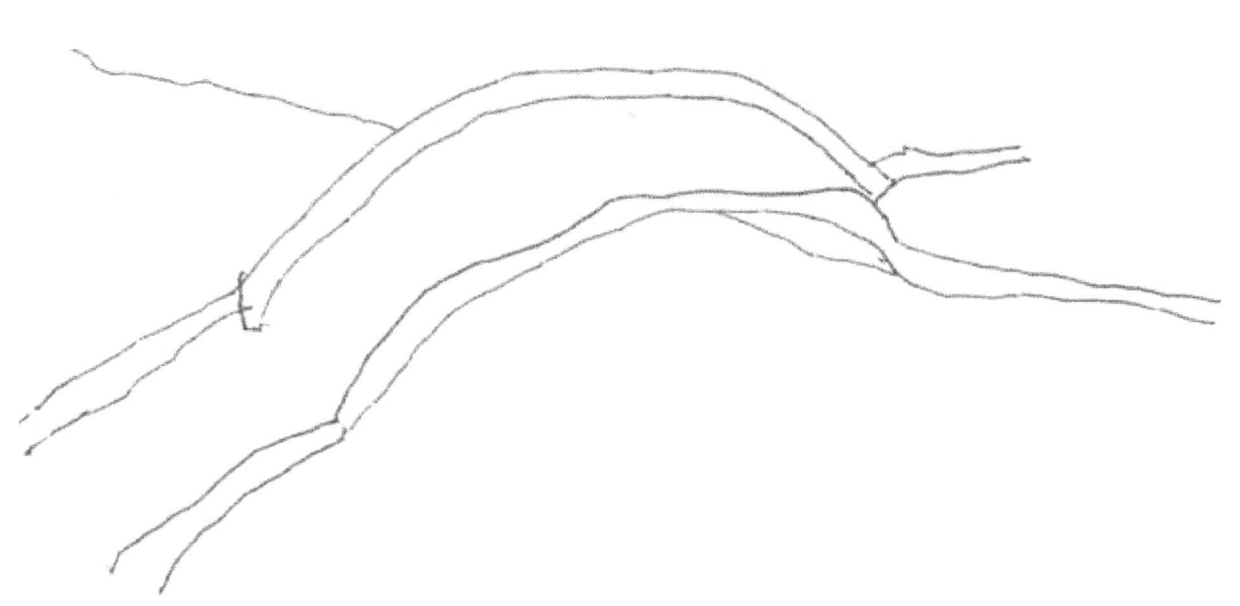

Will you cross a **BRIDGE**?

Color me BRIDGE

Will you Cross a BRIDGE?

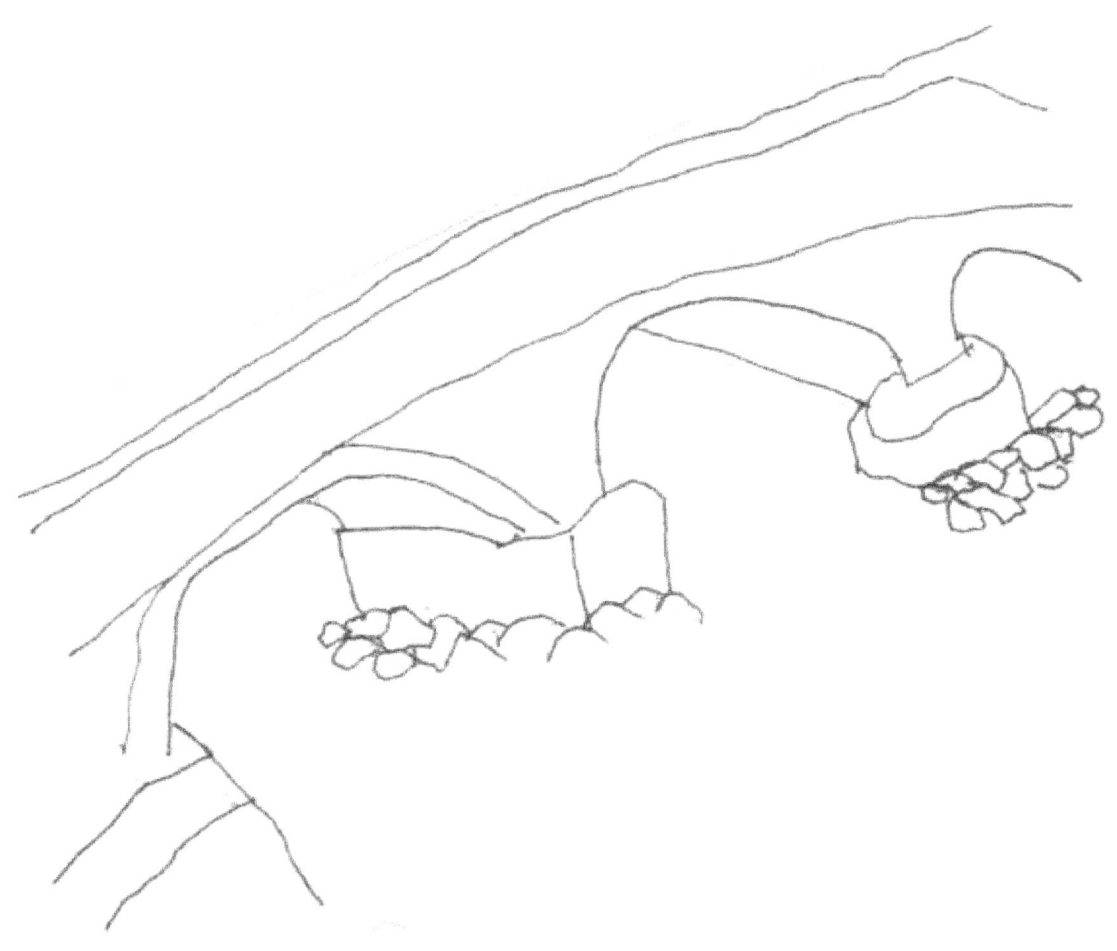

Discussion and Action

Preparation
Sharing the story
Exploring the question
With grace-filled people
And the journey
With Presbyterian Disaster Assistance

Preparation:

Create space in a room for coloring individual and large pictures using crayons and/or markers.

Tell the story:
A storyteller can tell the story of Noah

Let people choose small groups:

    a. The storm is coming

    b. It has been floating and safe.

    c. This space I'm in is crowded and we wonder where we'll end up

    d. The rainbow of God's promise is clear

    e. Something else

Pray.

Color as part of one large picture.

Take a break if the group wants.

A storyteller gathers us together and shares the story of Paul writing to the people in Galatia.

    a. It's comfortable being with people like me.
    b. It's difficult to cross a BRIDGE when we're crossing It.
    c. It's time to rest and figure out what is going on.
    d. I've crossed BRIDGEs before and know I can build a new one.
    e. The differences are great and it's scary crossing a BRIDGE.

Draw or add to a picture someone creates.

Cross a BRIDGE with Presbyterian Disaster Assistance (pda.pcusa.org) by hygiene kits, making school kits, of clean up kits.

Mail kits to PDA at the address they recommend.

www.ingramcontent.com/pod-product-compliance
Lightning Source LLC
Chambersburg PA
CBHW081800100526
44592CB00015B/2507